# The Millennial Renaissance

# The Millennial Renaissance

**HOW TO THRIVE FOR THE REST OF YOUR LIFE, EVEN THOUGH BOOMERS HAVE SCREWED IT UP FOR US. A RETIREMENT PLAN FOR MILLENNIALS AND BEYOND**

## Lucy Cohen

© 2017 Lucy Cohen
All rights reserved.

ISBN-13: 9781977808356
ISBN-10: 1977808352
Library of Congress Control Number: 2017915514
CreateSpace Independent Publishing Platform
North Charleston, South Carolina

## Everything you've been told about retirement planning is wrong

Maybe you haven't even thought about retiring yet. Maybe your parents haven't even retired yet. Maybe you have no idea how you would ever afford not to work when you're older.

Don't panic—you're not alone. Let's face it: most of us live paycheck to paycheck. How on earth are we supposed to even think about what happens when we hit sixty-five or seventy-five years of age?

Our generation has been somewhat ignored when it comes to sound advice around planning for the rest of our lives, which is why I decided to write this short book.

So who the hell am I, and why am I qualified to tell you that everything you think you know about retirement is wrong?

I'm Lucy Cohen. I'm an award-winning entrepreneur and business mentor. I'm currently thirty-four years old, and that means I'm a millennial. I can afford to "work" just three days a week and am on track to have enough money for a comfortable "retirement" by the time I'm fifty-two, possibly before. And I'm going to tell you how to do it too.

## A bit about me

I finished my A levels in 2001 and got a place to study drama at Exeter University. And then, at the age of eighteen, I had an epiphany: I realised that the future I had been sold of university, job for life, pension, and then retirement was a rapidly disappearing reality. All around me, my friends and peers were getting into heaps of debt at the age of eighteen. And few of them knew what they really wanted to do with their lives. They lived from loan payment to loan payment, were mainly terrible with money, and just assumed that everything would work out okay, because in the most part, it had for their parents.

Something didn't sit right in my mind with all this. I was about to run up a load of debt to gain a degree in a subject that had no obvious defined professional path after it. And all the adults around me were telling me that this was a good idea. At that time I thought that I wanted to go and work in film and TV. So I deferred my place at university and decided to take a year to gain some experience in this career I was so adamant I wanted.

Uh-oh.

I hated it.

I turned down my spot at university and, at the age of nineteen, decided that I wanted to build something that would support me for the rest of my life.

With university off the table (so much money, so few guarantees), I started looking around for what else I could do that would eventually let me work in a way where I called the shots. Freedom and financial security have always been very important to me, and I hated the idea of a financially uncertain future. I found out that I could do accountancy qualifications whilst I worked. I'd go to work in an accounts office in the daytime, and then one evening a week I'd go to college. Perfect! No running up debts, and I'd actually earn money whilst I worked. Why hadn't anyone mentioned this to me? Why had I never been told that this was possible?

That's not to say that it was a breeze. For three years I worked my butt off. I took every opportunity for extra learning, studied for every exam, and passed everything first time. As my skills and knowledge grew, I was becoming dissatisfied with the career progression I was experiencing. I wanted more autonomy, more freedom, and ultimately, more income. I started to think about how I could set up my own business with my newfound qualifications and experience. And as luck would have it, a very special woman came back into my life at just this time.

Sophie Hughes and I had been best friends throughout high school but kind of drifted apart when I went to a different sixth form than her. In the revision course for my last exam sat Sophie, having also taken a similar route to me in skipping university. Our friendship picked up where it left off, and pretty soon we'd gone into business together.

We spotted a niche in the market of small-business accountancy services. And over the years, we've been at the forefront of change in the accountancy industry. We took our skills and knowledge and combined it with our tenacity and drive to create something pretty revolutionary. We created Mazuma Accountants—the United Kingdom's first remote accountancy service for small businesses.

At the age of twenty-three, we had both started the wheels in motion for our retirement, even though we didn't really know it back then.

Eleven years on and we have offices in the United Kingdom, the United States, and Australia. We employ over twenty-five staff in the United Kingdom and provide our services nationwide. We have created a business model and structure that allows us both to be in the office just three days a week—giving us time to pursue other activities, interests, charity work, and money-making opportunities. We have also created enough residual income to allow us to put in place a plan for what happens when we reach retirement age. If all things go to plan, we'll be able to retire almost twenty years before the official state retirement age. And we'll have achieved a level of financial freedom well before that.

We've done this despite the financial crash in 2008, despite the credit crunch, and despite the fact that, as the media report, many of our peers are unable to afford deposits on homes and jobs for life, and final-salary pension schemes are almost a fantasy nowadays. Basically, we did it despite the boomers screwing it up for us all.

And we did all this with a few simple principles, a load of dedication and belief in ourselves, and not a degree between us.

If you're a millennial and you'd like to know how to create a fulfilling and financially secure future for yourself, then I'm about to tell you how.

Onwards.

# CHAPTER 1
## Let's Define Some Things

First things first—what is a millennial? And why do they need a retirement plan that differs in any way to the standard retirement planning advice?

**A millennial**

This term is thrown around a lot in the media. In short, it's a generation. The term "millennial" is broadly used to describe the generation of people who were born between the early 1980s and late 1990s to early 2000s. At the writing of this book, the oldest millennials are in their mid to late thirties, and the youngest are seventeen. Like every generation before us, we face challenges, but economically the world is a vastly different place to previous generations'. And the economic challenges we face are tougher and more uncertain than any generation before did.

Millennials are the generation who (according to research done by William Strauss and Neil Howe) are more civic-minded. We are confident, social, and team-oriented and use technology to interact and communicate with the world around us in a vastly different way to previous generations.

In 2015, the Pew Research Center conducted research regarding generational identity that said a majority did not like the "millennial" label—hardly surprising given the millennial-bashing narrative of current society.

As millennials we get a rough ride in the media. Barely a week goes by without us being blamed for something. Here are just a few ridiculous examples:

We've been blamed for a downturn in the manufacture of bars of soap. Because apparently preferring a body wash that isn't covered in germs is a heinous crime.

We've been blamed for a decreasing interest in real diamonds. Preferring ethical jewellery sources and having no money just isn't good enough for the diamond industry.

Blame even lies at our feet for killing off the good old suit. How dare we prefer to work in comfortable clothing!

According to the media, we are all work-shy, emoji-loving, suit-bashing, avocado-worshiping socialists who just need to grow up and start acting like adults.

The thing is, we *are* adults. So what's with all the hate?

The millennial generation is arguably the most socially minded and tolerant generation in history. We are the generation that ushered in equal marriage laws, elected the first black president of the United States, and created Facebook. And yet there is underlying tone to media coverage that we are lazy, entitled, and narcissistic. Why is this so? And maybe a more pertinent a question, if those things are even to a degree perceived to be true, what has created this generation, and what happens when they get old?

Well, one thing's for sure—the old rules don't apply to us, now or in the future. So what do we do about it?

We need a different plan for when we get old. Because we *will* get old, even if it seems a long way off right now. With the era of final-salary pensions and certainty of your age of retirement a distant speck in the rearview mirror, we need a plan.

So I have one. And no, it's not a "get rich quick" scheme—because they're all garbage (#sorrynotsorry).

This is a retirement plan written for millennials, by a millennial.

It's achievable and relatively painless to implement. Do it right, and you'll be able to have a fascinating and rewarding life, all the while looking out for the older version of you.

# CHAPTER 2
## What Is Retirement?

Let's pause for a moment and think about what retirement is. What image does it conjure up for you?

For me (and I'm sure many others), it conjures up the idea of not working anymore, giving up the nine-to-five, and living off the wealth you have accumulated during your life.

I think of bus passes, a mortgage that has been paid off, state and private pension income, and early-bird dining deals. For those who are lucky enough to take early retirement, I imagine a life of European holiday homes and linen shirts.

And the dictionary agrees (well, maybe not about the linen shirts). It defines retirement as "the action or fact of leaving one's job and ceasing to work."

Cool.

So let's agree that for the purposes of a useful definition, that's what retirement is.

We have a problem, though. "Retirement" in the traditional sense of the word is no longer a sustainable economic or social state.

The Office for National Statistics reveals some very interesting data.

The population in 2016 was at its largest ever, at 65.6 million and projected to reach 74 million by 2039. While it is growing, improvements in healthcare and lifestyles mean the population is getting older; in 2016 in the UK, 18% of people were aged 65 and over, and 2.4% were aged 85 and over.

As a result of the ageing population the old age dependency ratio (OADR) is increasing. The OADR is the number of people over 65 years old for every 1,000 people aged between 16 and 64 years old—in mid-2016 the UK's OADR was 285. It is a useful measure to understand how the balance in the population will change, particularly when planning for the needs of the different age groups...

The proportion of children in the UK population has declined from over 24.5% in 1976 to 18.9% in 2016. This proportion is projected to decline even further in future years.[1]

Can you see the problem here?

We have an ageing population. Put really simply there are more old people per young person who is working than there has ever been, and it's a trend that is set to continue. In terms of state pensions at least, it's the working generation that funds the retired generation. Effectively each working generation pays for the generation above them. So what happens when the retired generation's economic needs start to outstrip the resources provided by the working generation? Well, we see things happening as they are now—increases in National Insurance (swiftly u-turned this time around in 2017), increases in retirement age, and uncertainty about what we'll actually get when we reach state retirement age (assuming it hasn't been increased to ninety by the time we get there!).

So will millennials ever be able to retire in the traditional sense of the word?

Briefly, no.

To expand on that a little, my prediction is that some will, but most won't. And actually, that's okay, because we're not a generation that wants a mundane or mediocre life when we're older. We are adventurers and innovators. The idea of sitting around in my slippers and collecting the state pension seems shockingly dull.

So instead of having a retirement, I'd suggest we all work towards having a renaissance. It's a more feasible plan, and let's face it: it sounds a lot cooler too.

# CHAPTER 3
## Masters of Our Own Destiny

Let's start by redefining retirement. Let's reframe the idea of what being retired is—let's call it a renaissance.

The first step in creating your millennial renaissance plan is visualising what you think the later years of your life will look like.

Perhaps you'll take an adult gap year (or three) and head off travelling.

Perhaps you'll have a career change and run a B and B in the country.

Maybe you'll start a charity or community programme.

But whatever it is that you'll be doing later in life, you won't be relying on state handouts—because given the economic trends we've seen lately, that's foolish and naive. Sure, the state is supposed to be there to help us and look after us in times of need, but with all the political uncertainty in recent times, let's not assume that will be the case.

You'll need to think realistically about how simple or extravagant a life you want for yourself, both now and in the future. How much money you will need will hugely shape what your plans should be. If you want a simple self-sufficient life in the country, your financial needs will undoubtedly be less than someone who wants to live in a mansion in Beverly Hills. There's no judgement either way about what you choose—it's your life. But I would suggest being realistic.

Reality TV and shows that give people their big break into the entertainment industry have skewed people's ideas of how to achieve financial freedom and security. Sure, for the very few that big break happens. But for most of us, it never will. I really don't want to burst your bubble, but if you're waiting to get spotted and relying on that for your future, then you'll probably end up sorely disappointed and struggling financially.

The whole premise of the millennial renaissance is that we take control of things for ourselves. We don't want to be relying solely on the whim of someone else. It makes no sense to leave your future in someone else's hands when you have all the tools at your disposal to create your future for yourself. We need to row our own boats.

It's time to be masters of our own destinies and create a later life that reflects who we are and delivers us the lifestyle we want, without solely relying on the state or anyone else.

# CHAPTER 4
## Time to Get a Bit Angry

The media loves to tell us how we're not proper adults.

I'm tired of hearing this. Just because we like Instagram and street food doesn't mean that we are somehow not proper adults.

I'll avoid using the term "grown-up" because I think that suggests that someone has stopped growing as a person. And let's face it: none of us should ever try to stop growing as individuals.

So let's look at what the term "adult" means. I'm going back to the dictionary, and it defines an adult simply as "a person who is fully grown or developed."

Sounds dull.

Of course, in social terms the idea of being a proper adult has different connotations. It makes you think about owning a home, having a steady job, and maybe having your own children. Adults have pension plans, life insurance, and back gardens, right?

Well, you can kind of forgive the boomers and older generations for accusing us of not being proper adults, because they, for the most part, have a lot of those aforementioned things. They look at millennials with our house shares and gig economy and wonder when we're going to grow up and get a proper job or settle down and have kids—because that's what their parents told them to do, and that's what they went and did.

Of course, they're failing to realise that the traditional trappings of adulthood have been stripped away from us, made so inaccessible to many that they are an unachievable dream.

Take a look at homeownership. For many generations homeownership has been deeply embedded in the British psyche. Even today, 80 percent of people, when asked, would like to own their own home.[2]

In 1969 the average house price was around £4,000, and you'd have been able to own it when you were twenty-five.[3] As a comparison for a salary, in 1969 a teacher earned around £1,650 a year.

Nowadays the average house price is over £200,000—a rise that has hugely outpaced the incomes of those looking to buy houses. Again, comparing the salary of a teacher, in 2017 the average teacher earned £28,660. If you look at that in terms of being able to borrow multiples of your salary for a mortgage, you can really see the discrepancy between the two and the challenge that millennials face.

More than a third of UK houses are owned by households where at least one occupant is aged over sixty-five.

Already, 28 percent of those aged twenty-two to thirty years of age have been forced to remain at their family home or move back.[4] Statistics from the Chartered Institute of Housing (CIH) show that home ownership among twenty-five- to thirty-four-year-olds has plummeted from 67 percent in 1991 to 26 percent in 2013, whilst ownership among those aged sixty-five to seventy-four has increased from 62 percent to 77 percent. In 1981 this figure stood at just 49 percent.[5]

Give us a break! How are we supposed to own homes when the boomers have nabbed all the good houses at cheap rates?

Now let's move on to jobs.

Has any millennial ever got a job for life? Ever hear that term bandied around anymore? Nope, me neither. That, along with cheap housing and free university tuition, has disappeared. And this is a huge problem when we're being told that we need to grow up and be an adult. How are we supposed to plan for the future when everything about our futures is so uncertain?

My partner, an engineer, got made redundant three times in five years. Tales like this are not uncommon. Amongst your peer group, how many people have been in their job more than five years? I'd take a guess and say not that many. And not having access to a career with a ladder as our parents' generation did leads us on to the next problem.

## Pensions

I don't mean the state pension but private pension schemes. In the generations before us, far more people had access to final-salary pension schemes. These things were incredible! They gave you a guaranteed pension income based on what your final salary (or a calculation associated with it) was when you reach retirement age in that company. Just imagine that! Of course, these schemes are few and far between now—mainly because they are incredibly expensive to run. Some large companies offer something similar, but the payouts aren't nearly as good, and you'll almost certainly have to pay in more than the previous generation did.

So when we get criticised by the older generations for not being proper adults, is it any surprise that we don't even really try to get hold of what they have? They've taken all the cheap housing and scooped up all the good pension schemes, and they didn't have to pay for their tuition and retired before they were seventy. Oh, and in 2008 they ruined the economy for a bit.

The trappings of "adulthood" have been stolen away from us.

Let that sink in for a bit. Get a bit angry if you like.

Done?

Okay. We're moving on from that now. Being cross with the situation isn't going to change it. So we need to find ways to be more creative about how we achieve our later life dreams—and this is what creating your renaissance is all about.

Let's accept that home ownership and final-salary pensions are not on the table for most at this moment in time.

And now, like a true millennial, let's look at solutions to that problem.

# CHAPTER 5
# Do You Really Need That Degree?

**Is university worth it?**

We are a generation that has always been presented with a very clear path from school to university. Because that's what you have to do to get a good job, right?

Wrong.

Before I fully go into this, I want to caveat that there are loads of good reasons to go to university—life experience, fun, and learning. And for some people (like doctors), their profession requires university study.

But should absolutely everybody go to university? Hell no. There are loads of alternative options out there (like apprenticeships) that offer a totally viable career path without all the debt.

And yet university is pushed on young people as the be all and end all and has been for a while, despite the ever-increasing costs. When I did my A levels and our teachers spoke to us about what happens if we didn't get the grades we wanted, we were told about clearing. I remember being told that it's really a case of "bums on seats" for most universities, so you'd be bound to get a place on a course somewhere, studying something.

Erm...

Doesn't really sound like amazing advice given the economic investment required to go to university nowadays!

Let's look at the figures.

At the time of writing (with tuition fees recently being given permission to rise), the average cost of a three-year course in university is £53,000.[6]

Think about this logically. If someone asked you to invest £53,000 into a scheme whose success was entirely dependent on the work *you* put in for three years, and then at the end, you have no guarantee over what period you'd be expected to recoup your money—let alone make any money on top of it—would you invest?

I don't think I would.

But don't graduates earn significantly more over the course of their life? Maybe. This figure is proving hard to pin down, and studies suggest anything from £100,000 to £500,000 over the course of your working life.[7]

Assuming the lower end of the scale and a career of forty years, you're only earning an extra £2,500 a year on average. It would take approximately twenty years to recoup your initial investment—and that's not including the time spent not earning money during university, any time spent in a job where you're not earning enough to repay your student loan, or any additional money owed in loan interest. In economic factors, it's not really a great return on your money.

Now I am of course in no way saying that you shouldn't go to university. If it's what you really want to do, then you should absolutely find a way to do it.

But go in with your eyes open. Be smart about it.

We can no longer blindly trust the "wisdom" handed down to us by other generations. It's vital that we question everything if we want any chance of having a decent income in our later years.

So now that I've gone through some of the reasons why the world is such a challenging place for a millennial and I've told you that the best way of facing these challenges is to make a renaissance plan, I'm going to tell you how to do it.

And guess what—it's not all that hard to do!

# CHAPTER 6
## Adulting

Adulting is "the practice of behaving in a way characteristic of a responsible adult, especially the accomplishment of mundane but necessary tasks."

I was obviously going to have to do a chapter about this, especially given the flak that millennials get for not being "proper adults."

Despite the many reasons that I have gone through earlier in the book that mean we don't really feel like proper adults, unfortunately we still have to do some of the traditional adult tasks.

Getting this stuff done will give you the brain space to focus on the more important tasks required to live fully in the present and simultaneously build your future.

All this is the advice I give to my staff and mentees, and you are free to ignore it of course! But to my mind, it's absolutely crucial to make sure that you give yourself the best chance of success. For some people this stuff is just common sense and comes naturally. For others it's a real struggle to keep on top of the day-to-day. So here is a bit of life advice to get on board with that will help you lay the foundation for your renaissance plan.

## Routine and time keeping

This is critical if you want to lead a productive life. Everything in the world has a schedule. Your weekly yoga class has a start time. You'll have deadlines to pay bills, rules to follow to book doctors' appointments, and a time given to turn up at the dentist. The world has time frames and routines and things that have daily, weekly, monthly, and annual recurrences—and all variations in between.

You need to get on top of this.

## Don't be late for things

It is not cool to pay bills late, not just because all companies need money to pay their staff and your late payment might impact that, but also because it might wreck your credit rating. And having a crappy credit rating seriously affects your choices when it comes to borrowing money.

And it's not cool to turn up to things late. If you are the person who is perpetually late for everything, then you need to have a serious word with yourself. Granted, everybody is late *sometimes*; when there has been unexpected traffic or a home emergency you had to deal with, it is understandable that you are late. But if you are that person who is fifteen minutes late for everything, then I'm going to tell you some uncomfortable truths about yourself. Ready?

Your friends talk about you behind your back.

Yep. It doesn't feel nice to know that, does it? Imagine all your friends sitting around at a coffee shop, bar, or restaurant for lunch. There is an empty seat because you haven't shown up yet. They're hungry, but they can't order until you arrive. Some of them have other commitments they need to get to afterwards, which means that you are either going to make them late or they'll have to skip dessert and do that awkward thing of leaving some money or paying separately on their way out. And before you arrive, they're all saying things such as, "He/she is always late," "Sometimes I tell him/her to meet half an hour before we actually need to because he/she is always thirty minutes late," and "I haven't heard from him/her; has anyone had a WhatsApp?" And they're all joined together in really disliking the fact that you are always, always late.

Your parents don't respect you as much as they should. Of course, they would never admit this, but it's true. If you always turn up late to family gatherings or forget annual events and birthdays, then in their eyes you will forever remain a child. Psychologist Eric Berne came up with the parent-adult-child transactional relationship model in the 1950s. It explores the idea that we can switch between different states and roles in our interactions with people, sometimes even within one conversation. If you turn up late to something, your parents will instantly cast themselves in the parent role and you in the child role. They'll chastise you, and you'll sulk. And so the cycle continues! If you want to relate to them on the adult-adult plane, which is how I think all transactions should occur, then you need to get your routine sorted and turn up on time.

Your boss doesn't think you're serious about your job. This one should be really easy to get your head around. If you can't even be bothered to show up on time, why would your boss bother considering you for any opportunities that come up? Turning up on time is workplace 101. If anything, be early.

Being perpetually late isn't a personality quirk. It doesn't make you fun or interesting. It makes you an inconvenience. And it means that you are selfish and value your time more than everyone else's. There is no way that you'll be able to get on with your renaissance plans if you can't even sort yourself out to arrive on time or remember when to do things. That's really basic stuff.

### The solution to this is easy!

Thankfully, we live in a time where it has never been easier to make sure that you've got your life together.

We have at our disposal a vast array of planning, scheduling, and research tools. And most of them are in that smartphone in your hand.

Can't remember your dad's birthday? Put a recurring entry in your diary. And then sign up to a birthday-card delivery website where you can post him a card at the click of a button. An annual problem solved with about fifteen minutes of effort at the front end.

Don't know how long it will take to get somewhere? Google Maps. Then add twenty minutes in case of unexpected circumstances.

Crap at paying bills on time? Set up direct debits. And then pop the dates that things go out of your account in your diary.

Need to remember to do something? Literally anything? Put a reminder in your smartphone diary. My diary is full of little things that I have to do—phone calls I need to make, reports I need to run, appointments I need to keep, and even dates when my key staff are off work, so I know who is in the office.

It is so easy to be organised nowadays. I remember my dad having a little diary that he carried around with him when I was a kid. At the end of each year, he would go through it and copy over all the important things such as birthdays from his old diary into his new one—every damn year. In that sense, we have it so much easier than our parents did.

And that means that there is no excuse for not having your routine and timekeeping under control.

## Household chores

Dull. Dull. Dull.

But they need to get done. I am a firm believer in "tidy house, tidy mind." How can you ever expect to maintain focus and drive if your living environment is a mess? No one really wants to spend their time cleaning the bathroom or doing the laundry, but we need clean clothes and a clean loo.

So you need to develop a strategy to get on top of these things. And guess what—that's going to involve a routine too.

## Laundry

Pick a day and time that you do your laundry, and always do it on that day and at that time. For me it's 10:00 a.m. on Thursdays. I work from home on Thursdays and Fridays, but pick something that works for you. Before I was able to reduce my office hours, I used to load the washing machine on Thursday mornings and set the delay timer so that it finished around the time I was due home from work. If you have children, then you may need to do laundry more than once a week, so factor that in. But for me it's just my partner and me, and I am in charge of laundry (he's in charge of food shopping and cooking), so once a week is fine. I have a washing machine that has a rapid cycle, which is more than adequate for most things and is ecological too. I also have a condenser dryer for getting the clothes dry seeing as we can't rely on British weather to do that for us. The dryer is a very recent addition to my life, and honestly, it's a game changer. So, if you have space and the cash for one, I highly recommend it. And that's laundry done for me each week. I never run out of pants, gym clothes, or socks. I'm never in a panic that I don't have a certain thing that's clean. And most importantly, I don't have the mental drain of seeing a pile of laundry waiting to be done all the time.

## Food shopping

Do your food shopping online. I understand that budget can factor greatly into the choice of supermarket. I also believe that a couple of pounds spent on delivery will save you that and more in impulse purchases at the supermarket. And you'll also gain an hour or more back each week from not having to schlep around the aisles—an hour or so to be spent on more worthy pursuits. My partner does our food order on a Sunday night each week. We usually have it delivered on a Monday between 8:00 p.m. and 9:00 p.m. And that's another adulting job ticked off the list with minimal effort.

## Change your bedding

Change your bedding on a Sunday night. You'll sleep better in fresh bedding, and you'll feel a strange sense of accomplishment heading into Monday. I found that I was most productive on a Monday when I'd changed my bedding on a Sunday night. I know it's weird, but it works for me.

## Cleaning your home

For me, this is the worst one. In fact, I hated it so much that I got a cleaner who comes once a fortnight to do all the major things. If you can afford to get a cleaner, then there is no shame in doing that. You need to spend your time focusing on the activities that count towards your renaissance plans in some way. Spending a couple of hours per week cleaning may not be the best use of your time.

Think you can't afford it? You probably can. The cost of one takeaway meal a week pretty much pays for a cleaner. Decide what is more important to you if it's a choice between the two. Would you rather have that takeaway (that's gone in under an hour) every Friday night or not have to worry about cleaning your home? Whatever you choose, be comfortable with it. All that being said, I know some people for whom cleaning is a sort of meditation—cool! Two birds with one stone right there.

## Declutter

Stay tidy. Clutter is the enemy of productivity. It's a massive cliché, but "A place for everything, and everything in its place" is such a good life rule. If you can't even be bothered to hang your clothes up each day, how are you going to build a lucrative and comfortable future for yourself? If you claim not to have enough storage space for all your stuff, then you just have too much stuff for your current environment. Get rid of some things—I promise you probably don't need them all.

## Budgeting

Stop frittering your money away—seriously.

This is such a universal problem. We've all heard the sayings: "Money burning a hole in your pocket," "Spending money like water," and "Beer budget and champagne taste." They're all true. The whole point of this book is to help you build a comfortable life. And there is no way you're going to be able to do that if you can't get to grips with living to a budget.

Oh no! A budget!

News flash: hardly anyone in the world can afford every little whim and luxury that pops into their head.

Sure, it would be lovely to have that new pair of shoes to go to that event, because they'd really match your outfit, and everyone would say how great they are, and of course by extension how great you are. (That's how we get tricked into buying stuff.)

But do you need them? Probably not.

And when the event is over and you're living off ten pounds in the last week before pay day, those new shoes don't seem quite so alluring anymore, do they?

I'm not saying that you can't have nice things or treat yourself, but impulse purchases will be the undoing of you. It's so easy to buy things with one click, on the go, when we're not really thinking about it. I've done it too many times! Remember, buying stuff *won't* make you happy. Think before you click to buy.

In fact, you really don't need as much stuff as you think you do. Take a look at your wardrobe. I reckon you probably wear pretty much the same fifteen to twenty-five items of clothes most of the time. Be a bit creative. If you need a fancy outfit for a one-off event, don't buy it. Borrow it or rent it. And if you're pretty sure you'll never use something again, sell it and use the cash for something else.

## Save some damn money

A wise person once said, "You can't afford to buy something unless you can buy it twice." Or as Jay Z said, "You don't have a thousand dollars until you have two thousand." Translation: try not to spend all your cash each month. If you get to the end of the month and you have fifty pounds left, don't blow it. Put it away as savings, because guess what? Life happens, and sometimes we have to pay for stuff that we didn't expect to. I know, it sucks.

Thankfully technology can very much come to the rescue here. Apps such as Plum are able to save small amounts of money for you painlessly. It squirrels away one pound here, fifty pence there, and before you know it, you've saved a bit of cash for a rainy day.

## Check your bank account every day

This is a really simple way of staying on top of things and remaining money literate. I check my bank accounts every day. I know when things are supposed to come out of the account, and I can keep an eye out for delayed or pending payments that might skew my idea of how much money I have.

Not checking your bank account is like doing your food shopping without checking what you already have in the cupboards. It's stupid.

Checking your bank account every day also gives you the opportunity to check that everything is in order. I've known people who haven't noticed their card has been cloned until it was declined one day. In the meantime, the crooks had burned through their whole bank balance and overdraft. It takes a lot of time and a lot of stress to fix that sort of thing. Having a daily check helps you avoid that sort of drama.

I've frequently heard people say, "I'm scared to check my bank account." I get it; it's like the fear of stepping on the scales after an indulgent holiday. You know what, though? Not knowing how much you weigh doesn't make you any less heavy. And not knowing how much money you have doesn't make you any richer (or poorer). So don't bury your head in the sand—it really won't help you.

## Habits take time

Hopefully I've highlighted some practical ways that you keep on top of this adulting malarkey. Some days you'll be on top of it, and some days you'll inevitably slack or fall behind. Don't beat yourself up about it. Good habits take time to form. The key is to try to be as consistent as possible and teach yourself to do things even when you don't feel like doing them. Add things to your routine bit by bit. For most people, one of the easiest habits to get into is checking your bank balance—it can be done quickly on your smartphone whilst you're lying in bed trying to recover from your morning alarm going off. That's when I check mine!

Keep on top of the little things, and slowly and steadily you'll end up having created a myriad of great habits that will keep you focused, productive, and able to get on with your renaissance.

# CHAPTER 7
## Werk, Werk, Werk

Get ready to work hard!

Very few things in life come easy. And I do think that it's generally true that the things you've worked hardest for have the most value. A good analogy is going to a gig. If you've paid for a ticket, you're far more likely to turn up. That ticket has work and sacrifice associated with it—you've earned it. If you got that ticket for free, then it's really easy to skip the gig. I mean, what have you lost? You didn't pay for the ticket anyway. Over the years I've run many free workshops and seminars, and many where people have to pay. And guess what—the content was always pretty much the same, but people showed up to the ones that they'd paid for.

Earning something gives it value.

And to earn our future, we have to be prepared to work hard for our renaissance.

### Motivation is a myth

It's the third of January. You've had a skinful of booze and food over the festive period. You're motivated to make a change because you feel like crap, and none of your clothes fit anymore. So you do the classic New Year's resolution, and you get down to the gym and join up.

For the first few weeks, you're motivated. And then somehow life gets in the way. Other things creep in to steal your motivation. There's a family event on the day you usually do spin, so you skip the class. And you usually book in for the next class right after you've finished the last one, but you forget to because you weren't there this week. And then you don't really feel like going for the rest of the week either, because you're tired and work was busy. So you skip the rest of the week.

And Monday comes around again, and damn, you didn't book into spin last week so there are no spaces left now. And fast-forward to July, and you have a gym membership you never use, and you still don't fit into your jeans.

Such a cliché! And yet I'd guess that pretty much all of us have done it.

So why do we fail when we were so motivated to begin with?

Because motivation is a myth.

Sure, motivation pops up every now and again. And when it does, you should capitalise on it. But use it to tackle lots of little things, not one big thing. Motivation will not last long enough to get you through your everyday life. It will not really help you accomplish anything big in one go. And it will leave you crashing afterwards. When the motivation disappears, you're left with half-finished jobs and a feeling of shame and disappointment in yourself.

## Habits are better than motivation

What would happen if you had gone to the gym three times a week whether you felt like it or not? Reckon you'd feel better about yourself right now?

Habits are the backbone of building your renaissance. Habits are the things that mean you do tasks even when you don't feel motivated to do them. Instead of focussing your energy on trying to motivate yourself, just focus your energy on building in a few good habits into your daily life. They will keep you healthy and productive. Here are my top habits:

> Walk ten thousand steps a day (get an activity tracker if you don't already).
> Eat five portions of fruit and vegetables every day.
> Reply to all my e-mails by 4:00 p.m.
> Check my bank accounts daily.
> Go to the gym three times a week.
> Keep my home tidy.

And that's it. Those are the main little habits that keep me ticking over, healthy, and productive. They are good for my mental health as they allow me to achieve small tasks each day—and the achieving of those small tasks allows me to get on with all the bigger things I need to do.

Most importantly they instil in me the virtue of being willing to work hard. I can't achieve any of those little things if I sit on the sofa all day watching TV. So, in having to do all those things, I am creating an environment where I immediately reap the rewards of hard work. And that spurs me on to continue to work hard towards my renaissance plan.

## Time will pass

My final advice before you start on this plan is to remember that time will pass. In ten years' time, ten years will have gone by (well, duh). You can spend ten years doing nothing or spend ten years building something—that's up to you.

There is no point in not doing something long term because you can't think that far into the future or don't see the immediate benefit.

Time will pass anyway—you may as well get on with it.

# CHAPTER 8
## Your Renaissance Plan

So you've made it through the first part of the book, where we looked at why we need a different plan, and we've looked at all the attributes you're going to need to implement it.

If you're on board with all of those, then we can start thinking about how to create your renaissance plan, no matter what age of millennial you are.

Ready? Here we go.

### Get a job, and stick at it

Okay, this sounds really basic and not very groundbreaking, but please bear with me! You'd be amazed at the number of people I come across who have wasted a decade or more by not sticking at their job because it's not what they see themselves doing for the rest of their lives. As we've discussed earlier in this book, that idea of a job for life is pretty much dismissed nowadays.

You're likely to have two or maybe three different careers over the course of your working life. So what if you don't absolutely love your job right now?

The job doesn't need to be full time. It can be any number of hours you like and that works for you personally.

Why stay in a job that isn't what you want to do forever? Well, does this job provide you with income, human interaction, and good habits to do daily?

Unless you work for an absolutely awful employer who makes your life unbearable, then chances are your job isn't all that bad. And if you're in work, it's always easier to transition to another work—no awkward gaps on your CV or losing momentum because you've got out of the routine of keeping good habits.

I don't believe in dream jobs—they really don't exist for most people. But what can exist is a great balance of work and life if you have the right mind-set and apply the right tools.

Here's something that no one seems to tell you anymore: no job is perfect. I have a friend who is a doctor in A&E. She loves what she does, and she trained for many years at great expense to do it. However, some days are so tough, she wants to jack it all in for something less stressful.

Everyone feels like that sometimes. That's normal. That's part of being an adult.

Absolutely nothing is perfect all the time, so if you have a few bad weeks in work, don't quit, sulk, or whinge. Just chalk it up to experience, and take something out of it. Did it teach you to deal with a difficult person? Did you have to learn to make a hard decision? Did you have to work to the wire on a deadline? Good. All those experiences will make you resilient and prepare you for your renaissance plan. Embrace the tough stuff—it will make you better!

Do your job well, and give each task your full attention, even if it's not the most fascinating thing you've ever done. The simple fact of completing tasks to a high standard is a huge step towards creating your renaissance plan. We do the less interesting things well so that our lives can become truly fascinating.

And what do I really mean by "job"? By a job I mean something that gives you a regular and relatively predictable income. You're swapping your time and skills for money—someone else is paying you for your time and skills. By the time you have your renaissance plan in fully, you may not need a job, but for now it's a really good way to get on with life.

Having a job gives you an instant budget. It lets you know how much you can spend each month on accommodation, food, lifestyle, and savings.

Having a job also allows you to make contacts. You'll meet all sorts of people in the workplace whom you probably wouldn't meet (or even choose to meet!) in your peer group and social life. Observe these people, and learn from them. Interacting with all these people takes you out of the bubble of your age and peer group, and that's a really good thing.

## Get a pension plan

The other thing that traditional employment offers you is a chance to save into a pension. Now, I know I've discussed this idea earlier on and that the pensions of old just don't exist anymore.

But there are pension plans out there, and they can be worth saving into. I'm not saying plough thousands of pounds into it at a time, but creating a habit of saving small amounts of money into something long term is no bad thing.

All employers in the United Kingdom have to offer their staff something called auto-enrolment. It's a pension saving plan that is separate to the state pension (and yes, I think it's a glaring admission that the NI contributions are not enough to cover state pension requirements anymore, but that's a different topic). If you get the chance to opt in to it (or any other decent pension scheme), then you should. It's a small percentage of your salary a month, your employer will contribute to it too, and most importantly it's a big tick in the box for your renaissance plan. In just doing that, you've already created one or maybe two income streams for your renaissance—state pension and another pension.

## Buy a property

All right, don't spit your drink out. I know I've discussed at length all the reasons why homeownership is going to be tough for millennials. But I didn't say to buy a *home*; I said to buy a *property*.

Here's the catch though: you're not going to live in the property you own. You're going to rent it out and live somewhere else.

Some people think the idea of buying a property to rent out is a bit controversial. Is it hiking the prices up for other people? Is it inflating the market and contributing to the problem? In some cases, maybe. But let's face it: there will always be a market for people who want to rent properties, and there is no current reason why you can't kill two birds with one stone by buying a property to rent out.

Much of the problem in buying a home for yourself is that you have to have a big enough salary to guarantee you'll be able to pay back the mortgage company each month. And how much you are able to borrow will be a multiple of your salary. You'll also have to have a deposit to put down. And in many cases, the places that you want to live may be a bit out of your reach financially.

So why not get a rental property? It doesn't have to be somewhere you want to live or the type of property you'd want to live in yourself. This is a business opportunity for your renaissance plan.

Here's the idea: if you can't afford to do it on your own, find a property partner (or two), someone you trust and who will pull his or her weight when it comes to the legal side of things and dealing with issues as and when they come up. I suggest a long-term friend, sibling, or close family member who you won't fall out with. Save up a deposit together, and then buy one property together to rent out. If you both have a job, you have good credit ratings, and the property is a good prospect for rental, you should be able to pull this off.

Remember that this is a business deal—no emotion in this. This is transactional, and everyone involved needs to treat it that way. Get a solicitor to draw up contracts and do the legal stuff, and make sure that you all have wills in place to discuss what happens to the property if the worst happens.

Then you rent the property out for a decade or so, always making sure that this time frame is agreed well in advance with your property partner(s). In that time your tenants have had a great place to live, with good landlords who provide a safe environment for them. You are not tied to live in a property that you own, so you have freedom to move for work, life, or whimsy. Your tenants pay you rent, which pays your buy-to-let mortgage.

After ten years, you'll own a good percentage of that property. At that point you can decide to sell to finance a deposit on another property—maybe your home this time—or keep it and carry on if it's working out for you. But in whatever path you choose, you'll have some capital under your belt with a relatively minimal effort over the last ten years.

The housing boom of the early twenty-first century may not ever happen again. But even without that, house prices tend to go up in the long term.

You could even be more creative with this depending on how much of a deposit you can save up. What about commercial buildings? Shop fronts? Offices? Holiday properties abroad? All those things offer an opportunity for someone savvy to start creating some capital wealth for their renaissance. Think outside the box a bit.

## Get a side hustle

There was a time when people who took an extra job on top of their main work were looked down upon. It seemed to be regarded as an admission that your career wasn't going well or that you'd fallen on hard times. For me, I think it just makes good sense! The trick here is to weigh up what you are willing to spend some of your nonjob time doing in order to achieve your goals. There is no point in doing it if it's going to make you miserable—that's not the point of your renaissance. But what if you could use a side hustle to happily earn some extra cash and add something to your life?

There are the really obvious ones—work in a pub for two evenings a week, take a couple of shifts in a restaurant, and so forth. There's nothing wrong with these. They'll provide you with some extra cash, which you can use to put towards your renaissance or use to buy yourself extra experiences and things that your main job doesn't provide you with. You can use the income from these as an extra budget for frivolities or savings. It's not the most sophisticated way of doing it, but it has value and definitely helps you work towards your renaissance goals.

The point of a side hustle is that it gives you something extra. It improves your overall quality of life. And a side hustle is good at any age. All my grandparents have had side hustles. My granddad wrote books (not very successfully, but they made him happy and fulfilled him), and my grandma took TV and film extra work—there is always a need for a sassy old lady! My nan is eighty-four years old, and she's a piano teacher and also plays piano for the local ballet school. She's done that through her whole retirement and has allowed her to pay her bills with her pension and use her side-hustle money to feed her hobby, which is going off to watch tennis tournaments. *Vive la différence!*

So don't be scared of getting a side hustle if you need it or want it. It's savvy. It will open up opportunities for you both financially and emotionally.

## Build a residual income

Here's the biggie. This is where most of your efforts should be focussed for your renaissance. This one will take a bit more effort, but ultimately the rewards can be huge.

Let's spend a bit of time framing this. We live in a world where we are all constantly looking for more information—more things to scroll through on our devices, more interesting people to follow and learn about, and more content. Someone has to create all this content, and the people who do it best are reaping the rewards of it.

People are willing to pay small amounts of money for good content and entertainment. And if you get a lot of people willing to spend a small amount of money, you end up with a lot of money!

The trick here is that this has to be something that you already do, so that it doesn't feel like work. Unlike your job or your side hustle, you won't have set hours doing this. You'll be doing this all the time—living and breathing it. So you're going to have to make it something that you love; otherwise, you'll be miserable doing it, which defeats the whole point of your renaissance plan.

Be prepared not to make much off this in the first instance—this is a slow burner, but your passion has to remain high throughout. This is where my advice on habits rather than motivation comes into play. You need to get into the habit of living this new life—don't rely on motivation for it.

There are some good examples of the heavy hitters in this space. You have YouTubers like Zoella, who create YouTube videos on fashion and beauty. She has a huge following among preteens and has gone on to launch books as well as her usual YouTube offerings. At the time of writing, she is worth an estimated $4 million. And she created that for herself by living her passion and sharing it in an engaging way.

You have the Instagram stars like Julie Sarinana, who posts personal pictures of her daily style, which are viewed by her 4.6 million followers. Brands wanting exposure pay her up to £7,678 per post (at the time of writing).

And then we have podcasts. There are podcasts out there for all interests and covering pretty much every topic under the sun. Podcasts can make money through advertising if they're popular. But the income can also be fan-led. Patreon is a platform that allows fans of content to donate a small amount each month to their favourite content creators. Some Patreons ask for as little as a dollar a month, and that lets the creators get on with creating great content for their fans. In 2016 there were thirty-five creators who earned over $150,000 on Patreon. That's not too shabby for sharing something that you're already passionate about and would probably be talking about or researching anyway. Realistically there are many Patreon account holders who net themselves about $1,000 a month or so. That's a decent residual income, especially if you combine it with other income sources.

Some podcasts gain themselves a cult following. And that following allows fans to create their own additional revenue streams. The podcast *My Favorite Murder* is a great example of this. It's a comedy podcast created by Karen Kilgariff and Georgia Hardstark where each week they take their love of true crime and tell a story about a murder they're interested in. Sounds ghoulish, right? Wrong. If you're into true crime and comedy, it's absolute genius. (SSDGM for those in the know!). Not only has this podcast created literally millions of fans but also it's selling out stadiums for live shows and selling merchandise. And what's even cooler is that their fans (they're called Murderinos) have started crafting. Etsy is awash with gorgeous craft items being sold—all inspired by this podcast. The Murderinos have started creating their renaissance plan by crafting the thing they love to listen to, while the podcasters have created theirs by having conversations they'd have been having anyway, on air. If that's not a win-win, then I don't know what is.

Have you heard of fan fiction (a.k.a. fan fic)? Are you into writing fan fic? Or short stories? Services such as Ko-fi allow fans of your writing to give you tips when they like your work. If you love writing and gain a following, you could earn a great residual income from this. Again, just by doing the thing that you love anyway.

Finally, probably one of the oldest forms of a passive income in this arena is blogging. Most people are familiar with the name Perez Hilton. If you're not, he runs a controversial celebrity gossip website. In 2016 it was reported that he earned $575,000 a month from it. That's huge money, and that kind of success is definitely not the norm. But there are plenty of food bloggers out there who get some great perks from what they do. I have a friend who hasn't paid for a meal out in years because she gets so much free stuff from her food blog. With the money she has saved on dining out, she's been able to invest in other things. And she finds food blogging hugely rewarding on a personal level. That kind of deal is achievable if you put your mind to it and you do it about something you're already passionate about.

Now, creating a residual or passive income isn't easy. But if it's something you're already passionate about, then it's certainly in no way as taxing as relying on your job for your income.

## You're always a bit at work, and you're always a bit at home

Nowadays you can't just switch off at 5:00 p.m. and forget all about work. It just doesn't happen anymore. And think about it logically—when you're in work, do you only ever think and talk about work? No, of course you don't! You think about family and friends, and you chat with your coworkers about what's been on TV. So this idea of keeping work time and personal time entirely separate is a huge myth.

In my business, I accept that my staff have a lot of stuff going on. Social media and smartphones mean that they are always constantly connected with family and friends, even when they are sat at their desks working for me. And I don't mind that at all as long as their work gets done to the standard I expect. The trade-off is that when they are at home, they are always still a bit connected to work. They share messages with each other, update diaries, and send e-mails. Many of my staff are passionate about what they do, which is brilliant. But many of them see it as just a job, and that's fine too. I try to create an environment where they can all achieve their personal renaissance whilst I provide them with income security in return for them providing me with a good service, thus creating my income security. It's all one big circle to me!

The point I'm trying to make here is that when you start going down the route of creating a residual or passive income, you will always be in it. You can't switch off and have a break. It will always be there. Just like my staff, who do a bit of work from home in return for doing a bit of personal life in work, you will trade your down time for always being a bit in work mode. But if you do it right, the benefits are huge, and it won't feel like work. In fact, your ability to be constantly creating your own future will be hugely rewarding.

Time for a bit of a reality check at this point. I'd love it if you could all build yourselves a passive renaissance income of £1 million a year for the rest of your lives. But as I said at the start of this journey, this isn't a "get rich quick" scheme. This is about being real and creating something sustainable for yourself as you get older. The good news is that this can absolutely be done. And there are a few people who are already doing it.

# CHAPTER 9
## The Case Studies

In researching this book, I've been able to have some great conversations with people who are already thinking about and implementing their renaissance plan (whether they know they're doing it or not!). They are all at different stages, all leveraging different things. But what they have in common is that they are all bucking the traditional retirement-planning trend and creating a future for themselves that sees them being self-sufficient and fulfilled.

**Alan McDermott**
**Instagram: @nikemetconclub**

I had the chance to chat with Alan via e-mail (obviously e-mail. We're millennials; why would we need to meet face-to-face for this?).

Alan is the founder of the Nike Metcon Club. Yep, he started a club on Instagram for people who love Nike Metcon trainers—talk about a niche! He currently has over 105,000 followers, and this niche has opened up opportunities for him that wouldn't have been possible if he hadn't had the savvy mind to spot a renaissance opportunity. His background and job will surprise you!

*How old are you?*
Thirty-eight.

*Did you go to university, and if so, what did you study? And did you think, you'd have a career in a field associated with your degree?*
I went to the University of Glamorgan and did a degree in applied sport science. I have a career in health care, which I guess is vaguely associated with my degree, but if I'm honest, I don't really know what I thought I'd do with my degree. I just went to university because that's what everyone did. Later on I retrained as a dispensing optician, so I guess you could say my first degree wasn't really all that helpful!

*Do you have a "proper job"—that is, are you employed by someone else?*
Yes, I work as a dispensing optician.

*Is that job full time?*
No, part time. I realised that I wanted more freedom in my life and not be tied down to retail hours. So a couple of years ago, I decided to switch to part time and fill the remainder of my time with things that I enjoyed more!

*Do you have a pension scheme that you save into?*
No, and I don't think I plan to. There are more interesting ways for me to build my future or renaissance, as you put it!

*Have you thought about what retirement would mean to you and when you'd like that to be?*
As it stands I've not really thought about retirement plans in the traditional sense of the word—as in when that might be or at what age I might "retire." I don't think I'll ever really "retire," and that's more interesting to me than the traditional route. If I create income doing the thing I love, then obviously I will strive to continue that as long as possible!

*Do you do other paid work aside from your main job? And if so, what is it?*
Yes. I am a qualified CrossFit coach and do six to ten hours a week coaching, which I get paid for. It's great—I'm doing the sport I love, and I'm getting paid for it. I also find it really rewarding helping other people on their CrossFit journey.

*Do you own any assets or property?*
Yes—I own half a house with my wife.

*What made you start Nike Metcon Club?*
Really it was just the combination of a love of CrossFit and a love of sneakers! From an early age, I've been a big fan of shoes—I just couldn't afford them. I started purchasing CrossFit shoes and realised there was *no* information sources for an enthusiast, bar a few short articles online. I did some research, and there was no resource for any CrossFit shoes on Instagram, so I decided to start my account from there. It's a celebration of

the Nike Metcon trainer, and it's pretty popular—looks like I spotted a niche!

*How does it supplement your other income?*
I receive large discounts on shoes and apparel from companies that I promote posts for. That helps me afford more shoes! I also regularly receive free pairs regularly from these companies, so I guess you could say that's helping me not spend my own money, which I can then put into other things.

*What opportunities has it offered you?*
I have a very good relationship with Nike International; I'm in touch with the heads of Nike training in the United States regularly as well as the European arm. My relationship with Whatever It Takes (an international retailer) has meant that they are trying to create a job role for me to come on board on a more formal basis, but that is in early talks. I've potentially three or four trips coming up for launches and other events that I would never have been able to attend had I not set up the account.

*Do you think it has improved your quality of life?*
Right now in a monetary sense, not really. But in all other aspects, then it definitely has. I'm happy in what I do, and I'm really proud of the effect my account is having on the CrossFitsphere. I'm ultimately the go-to account for all things Nike Metcon now. It's a lot of hard work and can be quite challenging competing with rival accounts, but long term I think that this will provide me with opportunities that I wouldn't have had without it.

*Do you think that it could form part of a plan for your retirement? And if so, how?*
In truth, I hadn't thought about that until you approached me for this interview. But yeah, now I see that this can really open up some interesting opportunities for my future. I think that Instagram is the future of social media, so a job opportunity may come up with that, as I've proved I'm able to create great brand engagement for a singular product. Once at a certain level, my account could hold a rather large monetary value and could potentially be sold.

*Do you think that our generation needs a different plan for our retirement than say, our parents?*
Yes, for sure! There is a lot more opportunity for excess spending in comparison to the days of our parents and a hell of a lot less focus on saving or planning for the future. I suppose the earlier you plan it, the better, but when you're young, you don't think that far into the future. I know I didn't, and then, all of a sudden, you're pushing forty.

*What advice would you give to someone who wants to create opportunities for him or herself as you have?*
Trying to turn a hobby into a career takes hard work and luck. The luck is finding something that you love doing, that nobody else has done, but there is a market for it. Then sticking to it and building on that from there.

Alan has created a great opportunity here that really demonstrates the power of a renaissance plan. He's ticked several boxes:

- ✓ Job: part time
- ✓ Property: with his wife
- ✓ Side hustle: CrossFit coaching
- ✓ Residual income: Nike Metcon Club

If Alan continues to put his time and effort into creating his residual income while he has the financial prop of his job and side hustle, he's on track to create a great renaissance plan. And he's doing all this without working insane hours or sacrificing his relationships and social life. He's created a fascinating work-life balance.

Do you have a passion that you could leverage like Alan has? Could that be part of your renaissance plan?

**Aimee Bateman**
www.careercake.com

Aimee is an award-winning entrepreneur. Her story is a little different in that she's taken her passion and created a business around it. Her company, Careercake, is groundbreaking and a testament to the invention power of millennials.

*Tell me a bit about Careercake.*
Careercake is an award-winning e-learning platform, offering e-courses within areas relating to job-hunting and career development. We have approximately five thousand individual users to date in over thirty-two countries.

*How did your business start?*
I spent over a decade as a commercial recruiter, but when the recession kicked in early 2010, I found many talented people out of work through no fault of their own. As a recruiter, I felt limited in the ways I could help them. We are employed by the company, and unless the job seeker matches our brief, we can't help them. I wanted to help, so I bought a fifteen-pound secondhand camera on eBay and started making YouTube videos in my living room—short videos that would help people in all areas of job hunting, CVs, interview, how to write a cover letter, and so forth.

Within a short amount of time, my videos had received thousands of views, and I was approached by BBC Learning and other organisations to work with them as a consultant and careers speaker.

To date my videos have twenty-four million views across seven strategic partner channels on YouTube, and I took private investment in 2015, to turn the YouTube videos into high-quality learning videos within our own comprehensive reporting platform.

*Did this start as a side hustle?*
Yes, you don't make money from just making YouTube videos. I kept my job for about six months until my side hustle allowed me to pay my mortgage and phone. It was still struggle, and I did lots of part-time (less stressful and less paid) jobs, but my key priority was "could I pay my mortgage?" and as soon as the answer was yes, I quit.

*How old are you?*
Thirty-six years old.

*Have you had previous careers? If so, what were they, and how successful were they?*
I have always worked as a recruiter. I had a small lifestyle business when I was twenty-four years old (nothing to do with recruitment or careers) that was a total disaster, but I learnt a lot about myself and about business—lessons that help me now in my current business.

*Do you have a traditional pension?*
I have no traditional pension. By nature I'm very high risk, and I see my money working better for me in other areas right now.

Putting money back into my company is me basically betting on myself, and I feel safer doing this.

*Do you own a property?*
I own a property, and the mortgage will be paid off on that in about twelve years. I rented it out for a bit, but it is where I live now. I don't plan on selling it and will rent it out when I buy my next home.

*What do you see your "retirement" looking like? Do you have a specific retirement plan?*
I see "retirement" as financial freedom. I see this happening within the next ten years, due to development with my company. I don't see retirement as "not working." I will always work for myself, not because I need to earn money, but because I want to.

*What advice would you give to anyone looking to carve out a niche for him or herself?*
Don't work to improve your weaknesses. Identify what you are good at.

Drop the things you are terrible at. Accept them, and move on.

Pick one thing you are good at, and put everything you have into being crazy awesome at that.

Being okay at lots of things is too risky in this competitive marketplace.

You have to have one thing that you are untouchable at; then you will always win.

*Did you go to university (what did you study if you did)?*
Yes, I did a marketing degree.

*Is your career now anything to do with what you studied if you did?*
I would say yes; even though I employ a great marketing manager, I have a clear knowledge of the subject.

*If you had your time again, would you go to university?*
Yes, I would. But not because the subject matter was essential; more on a personal level.

So that's Aimee!

Her path is slightly different to Alan's. She's more about investing everything in her business to gain financial freedom. But she still ticks some really interesting renaissance-plan boxes:

- ✓ Job: her company
- ✓ Property: will be owned fully in twelve years
- ✓ Residual income: her company and future plans for renting out her property

Just like Alan and me, she doesn't think she'll ever "retire" in the traditional sense of the word. She's all about the renaissance plan—creating financial freedom by doing the things you're passionate about.

Are you entrepreneurial? Would you be able to work for yourself? If so, perhaps that could be a great way to start your renaissance plan. Why not back yourself instead of backing a traditional saving plan?

## Dr. Emil Hodzovic
### Instagram: @ProjectGoliath

Dr. Emil Hodzovic is a really interesting case study. A qualified doctor and fitness fanatic, he's created a personal brand that has developed over the last six years. Alongside a challenging and demanding career choice, he's built a brand, nutrition and fitness business, and financial opportunities by carefully sharing his story of competing in strongman and bodybuilding competitions. Along the way he's gained a following of fans through his online persona, Project Goliath.

*Tell me about what you do.*
I am an emergency doctor. I no longer work within the typical framework of the NHS since I left two years ago and just work ad hoc shifts (locum) entirely. In the current state of affairs, I could work full time if I wanted to, but I use it to give me the flexibility to allow me to balance my medical work with my other passions within both fitness and medicine.

Within fitness, I am a nutrition-and-fitness coach, and I combine this with my medical background to optimise people beyond what a doctor or fit pro can do on their own. On top of that, giving up full-time NHS medicine has allowed me to expand my scope of practice within medicine.

*How old are you?*
Thirty years old.

*Do you own a property?*
Yes, I own a house that I live in and have a mortgage on and also have two buy-to-let flats that I have recently acquired.

*Did you go to university?*
Yes, Cardiff University, Medicine MBBCh 2005–2011, and UWIC, Sports Exercise Science 2008–2009.

*Is your main work related to what you studied?*
Yes. "Main" is a difficult phrase, as I do a lot, but most of my income comes from work related to my medical degree, yes.

*Is your secondary work related to what you studied?*
Yes, as in both the secondary medical and fitness stuff.

*What made you start Project Goliath?*
Project Goliath was initially my blog about my journey to become a strongman (literally—my project to become Goliath) back in 2011 just before I started work as a junior doctor. Starting full-time NHS work was jarring to my accustomed lifestyle, and very quickly I realised at this stage I couldn't balance it with high-level competition, and so I stepped back from strongman, allowing medicine to take priority.

Then three years ago, when I decided I wanted to make a comeback into fitness (and had fallen out of love with medicine), I initially attempted to rebrand to what I thought may be a more marketable name, but after a period of time debating back and forth, I decided to just stick with it. From there it grew as my pseudonym within fitness and allowed me a little anonymity, separating my work as a doctor with me posing in my pants. PG was a blog that became a pseudonym and social-media handle and now is basically what I operate under within fitness alongside my name.

*Do you have any formal retirement plans?*
I have four years' worth of NHS pension, and that is now no longer being contributed to. I am currently getting into property that I am planning to use to fund my retirement.

*Does your social-media presence add value to your life either financially, via other benefits, or in any other way?*
Social media has allowed me to leave medicine and get into fitness and to the position I am in today. It allowed me to grow my online presence and therefore client base while working as a full-time doctor to eventually allow me to leave entirely.

Now that I am here, it has provided me with all my sponsorship opportunities (free stuff, exposure, shoots, and events) as well as allowing me to network and pass on my information to a potential client base. In that regard, I get a lot of my clients through social media but also through word of mouth. In these cases, when I am mentioned as a potential coach, my social-media presence acts as an online CV for people considering coaching with myself.

Social media is a bit of a double-edged sword in terms of the falseness and idyllic image that it puts out (I do try to keep it real as much as possible), but it has also allowed me to pursue everything I have achieved up until now within my life and still plays a large role.

*Do you agree that our generation needs a different sort of retirement plan to previous generations? What are your thoughts on this?*
I agree 100 percent. Standards and expectations are much higher, we're living longer, and jobs are less secure. There is a lot

of delusion and people looking for a big break now that social media makes this appear more accessible, and people end up skipping the bit where they gain skills or a job or any real-life assets and end up stuck.

For me personally even if I worked within the NHS for forty-plus years and had a full pension, I would always look to have backup plan and top up. My current situation means that I have to consider this backup plan as my new main source of pension, and I think in that regard I am lucky. I went from a secure job with an excellent built-in pension to one with no security and no future planning. This meant that securing my income and future was in the forefront of my mind in whatever I ended up doing, whereas I think of lot of people, especially within fitness, don't consider these things until it is far too late.

*Have you thought much about retirement plans? Or if you'll ever truly retire?*
I have a plan that in ten years (when I am forty), I will not *need* to work (so retire?). For me that means I can continue to do what I want to do for the rest of my life without any pressure or fear for financial insecurity (and regain the stability that I lost by leaving medicine). I love my work, so I find it highly unlikely that I will actually retire and stop working, but, for example, it would allow me to travel and not worry about my income month to month or year to year or even beyond that.

*Do you see social media as a way of people creating added value in their lives? If so, how?*
Social media is a tool, and if used correctly, it can change your life. However, for the vast majority of the population, it is

misused and abused, and people lose out. It puts out a false image and makes people feel like crap because they aren't "perfect." People are bombarded with these images from apparently normal people, and a lot of it is largely false or engineered to look infinitely better than it is.

So yes, it can add value to people's lives, but a lot of people are both addicted to it and feel worse overall because of it. There is also this phenomenon of people taking it "seriously" to become the next thing and actually not developing any sort of real-life plan. They are looking for their break to become "insta-famous" (whatever that means—often they have no plan in the blind race to acquire more followers, even buying them, which surely defeats the point in the whole endeavour?).

It's all a bit upside down. All my social media is professional and business orientated. Prior to starting back up within fitness, I got rid of all my personal social-media accounts and had a few-month hiatus from social media entirely to ensure to myself that I wasn't doing it to feed my ego. I don't put any personal information up on it nowadays (birthdays, relationships, etc.), and I rarely browse or check it—only to post content and interact with comments, and so forth. I look forward to the day where I no longer need it and can shut it down (or have someone else run it for me), once it has done what it needs to do.

*Do you think that in the future people will be able to earn an income from their personal brands created via social media? If so, how might that look?*
I think that people will always be able to earn money from social media, but the market is so saturated that, as with anything, only the top 1 percent (or less) will make it. Whether this

is through promotion of their real-life businesses, driving traffic to websites, being paid for advertising by sponsors, or even directly selling, I think it will continue to grow.

And that's Emil!

Dr. Emil Hodzovic is really ticking a lot of the renaissance-plan boxes. And he's proof that even with a demanding choice of career, you can start to build something that will service you for the rest of your life. Just like Alan and Aimee, he doesn't believe he'll ever truly retire in the traditional sense of the word, but he's working towards financial freedom and a path that will allow him to pursue other activities like travelling.

- ✓ Job: medicine (now part time)
- ✓ Property: own home and rental properties
- ✓ Residual income: Project Goliath

So could *you* take the thing that you love and share your experience with the world? Could *you* combine that with a career and use the two to create income and investment opportunities?

Of course you can!

### Sheri Miles

**Instagram: @sheri__miles** (two underscores in the handle!)

Sheri's case study is ever so slightly different. She isn't actively creating her renaissance just yet, but she has the qualities and habits of someone who would be easily able to do so. Sheri is an international-level powerlifter and keen pole dancer. She showcases her powerlifting and pole-dancing hobbies to great effect via social media and has gained herself quite a following that she could potentially harness as part of her renaissance plan if she were to choose to.

*Tell me about what you do.*
I work as a regional service manager for a medical devices company called Olympus. I manage a team of four people who cover hospitals over half of the UK; my team provides training and support on clinical use and maintenance of flexible endoscopes. I am on the road a lot, travelling, and I occasionally have to travel overseas.

Powerlifting and pole dancing are my hobbies. I started pole dancing about five years ago; the reason I started was to get fit as I hated the gym! Then I got hooked. I started powerlifting about two and half years ago after joining the gym to get stronger at pole dancing. A PT at my gym at the time recommended it to me when he saw I was strong.

*How old are you?*
Thirty-one years old.

*Do you own a property?*
Yes, a two-bedroom semidetached house that is my home.

*Did you go to university?*
Yes, Kingston University, Greater London.

*Is your main work related to what you studied?*
It's kind of related but not directly. I studied paediatric nursing at university; however, I am not a nurse. I work in the medical sector for a private company.

*Is your social-media content usually related to what you studied? If not, what is it about and why?*
No, my social media is related to my powerlifting hobby and pole-dancing activities. I share my powerlifting as a visual and public diary, great for tracking progress and sharing with the community, and the same for pole dancing. Sharing hobbies is a great way to connect with other people who have the same interests.

*What made you start focusing on social media for promotion?*
I wanted to connect with other people who have the same interests as me, and it's also useful to keep myself accountable for my progress. I find that sharing my powerlifting training videos and planned upcoming events keeps me on track; as sharing it with the public gives me the mind-set that I have to see it through.

*Do you have any formal retirement plans? (Traditional pension, employer pension, savings, etc.)*
No savings, unfortunately. I contribute to a pension scheme through work, and that is it!

*Does your social-media presence add value to your life either financially, via other benefits, or in any other way?*
Due to my active Instagram account, I have received the odd freebie—a few powerlifting items from Mark Bell and some free clothes from a pole-dancing clothing company. It hasn't added to my life financially. However, I have met people through Facebook, and I have gained lifetime friends from networking and sharing my hobby. Social media has enabled me to become well known in the powerlifting community.

*Do you agree that our generation needs a different sort of retirement plan to previous generations?*
Yes, we are living longer, and living costs have escalated. People are living more in the "here and now," relying on credit with high house prices or rent and bigger mortgages. Monthly salaries are more stretched, which makes it more difficult to save with less disposable income available. Interest on savings accounts is in no way as good and rewarding as they were back in the day, so the incentive to save is less for most people.

Many people in the previous generations used property buying as a retirement plan, which I believe has had an overall negative effect on new generations looking to buy property to live. I don't believe property buying and reselling as a retirement plan is a good option or even feasible for this generation, and saving is tough due to the points I mentioned previously, so alternative options should be considered at a younger age.

This generation is one of job hoppers, which can lead to an uncertain future and less security. A retirement plan is probably low down on the priority list of everyday living and getting by.

I have no idea of how this can be revamped to suit our current lifestyles, but I do agree a different approach is needed.

*Have you thought much about retirement plans? Or if you'll ever truly retire?*
I have not given this any thought! I very much live for the moment. I have an attitude that makes me think I will deal with the next stage in life when it comes, and I don't necessarily think this is sensible or the right attitude towards it! But I would like to retire at an age where I can enjoy it and not work into my seventies!

Because I haven't made any retirement plans or really thought about it, I believe I will be in some form of work until I can no longer work anymore. My other option would be to be a lady of leisure when my husband eventually takes over more responsibility at his job (the lady-of-leisure option is very unlikely for me—I like being busy).

*Do you see social media as a way of people creating added value in their lives? If so, how?*
It definitely provides an excellent network profile to meet new people. If you have the ability to market yourself well, I believe that you can attract things such as sponsorship, which leads to events and other social perks. On the flip side, it can also be negative; I think that it's quite easy to waste hours of a day scrolling and looking at other people's lives, which adds nothing to your personal life.

And that's Sheri!

As you can see, even though Sheri hasn't formally thought about her future-life financials or made specific plans towards it, she is already exhibiting many of the traits of someone who can make a successful renaissance plan. Sheri is a great example of what I'm sure many people out there are already doing—she has the skills and an interesting story to tell; she just hasn't quite got it all in line yet.

- ✓ Job: medical device company
- ✓ Property: home
- ✓ Pension: via her employer
- ✓ Fascinating hobby: powerlifting and pole dancing

Perhaps you already have the basis of a great renaissance plan, but you just don't know it! And that's really the joy of this mind-set. Like Sheri, putting in a great plan wouldn't take a huge amount of effort over and above what she is already doing. Could you do the same? Well, of course the answer to this is yes—you absolutely can!

# CHAPTER 10
## Get On with It

We've looked at the whys.
We've looked at the hows.
It's time for the nows.

No matter what age you are when you're reading this, there is absolutely no better time to start working on your renaissance plan than right now. And if you feel like you've fallen behind on life stuff, for whatever reason—it doesn't matter. This is a plan that can be implemented no matter what age you are.

Old age is going to happen to us all—we can't get away from that. It's vital that we set in motion plans to make sure that our later life is just as fascinating and fulfilling as our younger lives have been.

So go and do something right now that will help you towards it. Set up some savings with a savings app or tidy up your house. Do something, right now.

Start creating good habits this very moment.

Start thinking creatively about what your niche can be. What do you want your life to look like right now? What is the combination of job, savings, side hustle, property, and passive income that will create your ideal renaissance?

What do you want your future to look like? What is it that you want, and how much money will you need to achieve it?

Change doesn't happen overnight. Remember that this is a long-term plan, not a "get rich quick" scheme. Your renaissance is worth putting the effort into for the long haul. As I said earlier on, time is going to pass anyway; you may as well be getting on with it!

My final advice would be to do something every day that benefits present you and builds something for future you.

Good luck, and have a happy renaissance!

## ENDNOTES

1. "Overview of the UK Population: July 2017," The Office for National Statistics, last modified July 21, 2017, https://www.ons.gov.uk/peoplepopulationandcommunity/populationandmigration/populationestimates/articles/overviewoftheukpopulation/july2017.

2. "Housing Aspirations," Ipsos Mori, last accessed October 10, 2017, http://www.ipsos-mori-generations.com/housing.

3. "Homeownership: The Generation that Had It so Good," *The Guardian*, last modified August 4, 2015, https://www.theguardian.com/money/2015/aug/04/homeownership-the-generation-that-had-it-so-good.

4. Chris Belfield, Jonathan Cribb, Andrew Hood, and Robert Joyce, "Living Standards, Poverty and Inequality in the UK," Institute for Fiscal Studies, last modified July 2014, https://www.ifs.org.uk/uploads/publications/comms/r96.pdf.

5. "Young People and People on Lower Incomes Paying the Price for Our Broken Housing Market," The Chartered Institute of Housing, last modified March 9, 2015, http://www.cih.org/news-article/display/vpathDCR/templatedata/cih/news-article/data/Young_people_and_people_on_lower_incomes_paying_the_price_for_our_broken_housing_market.

6. Harry Glass, "Student debts to escalate as average cost of three years at university soars to MORE THAN £53,000," This is Money,

last modified August 15, 2012, http://www.thisismoney.co.uk/money/studentfinance/article-2188668/Student-debts-escalate-average-cost-years-university-soars-53-000.html.

7. Elizabeth Anderson, "Graduates Earn £500,000 More Than Non-graduates," *The Telegraph*, last modified July 16, 2015, http://www.telegraph.co.uk/finance/jobs/11744118/Graduates-earn-500000-more-than-non-graduates.html.

**ABOUT THE AUTHOR**

Lucy Cohen is an award-winning entrepreneur, business mentor, and millennial based in South Wales in the United Kingdom. *The Millennial Renaissance* is her first book.

Printed in Great Britain
by Amazon